PREDESTINATION

by

Howard G. Hageman

A FORTRESS BOOK

FORTRESS PRESS   •   PHILADELPHIA

Printed in U.S.A.   *UB2014*

Foreword

The need for putting what we, as Christians, believe into words everybody can readily understand poses a constant challenge. In response to that challenge the New Testament itself was written in a language commonly spoken and understood. Through the ages handbooks, catechisms, and tracts have been written and, since the invention of printing, published to meet the need for clarifying in every age what it means to be a Christian.

Whether it is more difficult to be a Christian in one age than another is hard to say. But being a Christian in the second half of the twentieth century is becoming more and more complicated. This heightens the challenge of spelling out for our day in an uncomplicated way what it means to be a Christian. To put the thought patterns of theology into terms that are readily understood is not easy. Yet saying what we believe in such a way that others, without too much difficulty, will understand what we are talking about is the test of our own grasp of what we believe and hold to be true.

In tackling this task the authors of Fortress Books do not try to make a difficult faith seem easy but to make it easier for the reader to see how demanding Christian discipleship really is and how important it is for him to give meaning to what he believes in what he does. And so the authors want to give the reader clues to guide him in making his decisions from day to day. It is the hope of the publishers that these small books, dealing with central themes of Christian faith and life, may succeed in their purpose.

Helmut T. Lehmann, Editor

TO THE REAL JAN

in appreciation of the questions
he has asked, though he never did
ask this one!

DEAR DR. HAGEMAN,

Please forgive my breaking in on your vacation. But in preparing some programs for our young people next fall I have been reading over various historic confessions of faith. They really have me upset! Though I have been brought up in church all my life, I never knew that there were still churches that were officially on record as believing in the whole business about predestination and election.

It strikes me as incredible that in this day and age any church can still profess to believe that God arbitrarily and for no good reason saves some people and sends others to hell, regardless of who they are or what they do. Of course, I knew that such ideas had been put forward long ago, at least by John Calvin. But I had always assumed that the whole grim notion was peculiar to him. Surely nobody takes that seriously any longer—certainly not in modern times.

Do you think we have to take it seriously? If not, why do we continue to preserve such language? Monuments to the past are all well and good, but I think we ought to have the honesty and courage to quit carrying about the relics of an entirely outmoded theology, especially when it could be troublesome to so many people. Please do not think I am a heretic or a crusader. I am simply puzzled. I would like to know why the church seems to insist on complicating the Christian faith with such an impossible article of belief.

Very truly yours,

JAN

1

DEAR JAN,

Your letter indicates that you were shocked to discover that in this day and age "any church can still profess to believe that God arbitrarily and for no good reason saves some people and sends others to hell." I am not sure how good a description that is of the traditional Christian doctrine of predestination and election, which is what is bothering you. What bothers me is the fact that you were brought up in church all your life without ever realizing before this what an essential role these doctrines have played in Christian history. The fact that they have become the dead letter that you suggest may have something more to tell us about the life of the church than about the doctrines themselves!

To answer your question about how seriously we must take all this will, I suspect, take more than one letter. So in this one let me limit myself to an attempt to give you a little better historical perspective.

You single out John Calvin as the real culprit in this business and at least imply that predestination was his idea. Well, that John Calvin believed in it no one can question. But I have never been able to understand why this doctrine, which has occupied a central place in Christian thinking for centuries, should be labeled "Calvinism" as though John Calvin had thought it up and nobody but his disciples ever took the doctrine of predestination seriously.

For the moment I shall skip over the various bases for it in the New Testament, though we shall certainly have to look at them before we are through. So far as I know, the first (and in many ways one of the most thorough) presentations of the doctrine was in the works of Augustine. What may surprise you more is the large place it has in the writings of Thomas Aquinas who, as you know, is still the standard theologian of the Roman Catholic church. All that I am trying to say is that predestination had a long history in Western Christendom before the Reformers appeared on the scene.

And as far as the Reformers themselves were concerned, Zwingli and Luther believed in predestination every bit as much as Calvin did. Did you ever read Luther's little pamphlet on the freedom of the will, *De Servo Arbitrio?* Get it and read it some time. Even though its more extreme statements will not be found in the classic Lutheran confessions, it will convince you that predestination was an idea which Luther took seriously.

Of course there were differences between the Reformers. But I should argue that they were differences in emphasis. Luther was, after all, the pastor and the preacher. Calvin was more the systematic theologian. The result was that Luther's statements are more limited in their scope. It was the biblical and evangelical aspect of the doctrine which appealed to him. The treatment in Calvin is far more complete and systematic. In fact, some people would argue that it is too complete and too systematic, drawing conclusions which theologians before him had refused to draw.

I don't know whether that is true. But I do know that it is not important. When it comes to affirming their faith in the predestination and election of God Luther and Calvin and Zwingli all speak with one voice.

The only point I wish to make in this letter is that the doctrine of predestination is no Calvinist monopoly. We may find it disagreeable. But we have to acknowledge the fact that it has been part of the mainstream of Christian thinking at least since the time of St. Augustine. (Once again I am for the moment deliberately passing over the New Testament witness.) Since that is the case, it is not quite so easy to be rid of as you suggest. If it had merely been Calvin's notion, we might follow your suggestion. But since it has been pretty much of the fabric of Western Christian thought, Roman Catholic and Protestant alike, we cannot dispense with it quite so glibly.

In fact, your suggestion prompts me to a counter one. Don't you think you had better find out just what it is you are getting rid of before you consign it to the scrap heap of outworn ideas? ~

Sincerely,

2

DEAR JAN,

I am sorry for the way I ended my last letter. It was unkind of me to suggest that you did not really know what the doctrine of predestination is. But I hope before we are through to be able to show you that it does have some rather surprising implications that are not always evident when we first begin to think about it.

Clearly, however, we are not going to get to that in this letter. For you have raised another historical question by asking me whether the tradition which I mentioned in my last letter has been all of a piece. Have not Augustine, Aquinas, Calvin, Zwingli, and Luther had their opponents within the church, and has the church ever really decided the question between them?

The answer, of course, is that from the time of Augustine on there have been Christians who have been opposed to the doctrine of predestination, at least in some of its forms. Augustine's opponent was a man named Pelagius. I suppose no one has ever opposed the doctrine of predestination more thoroughly, for Pelagius maintained that man was a completely free creature, able to decide for or against God entirely of his own free will. His opinion, incidentally, was condemned and nobody in all the long history of argument that followed ever tried to maintain it.

I think we shall have to take Pelagius' ideas up later on because they are the form in which most people who oppose the doctrine of predestination today try to do it.

But the history after Pelagius is the story of attempts to find some middle ground between the two positions of predestination and free will. Thus after Pelagius' condemnation, there was a group of theologians called "Semi-Pelagians." Or, while I know little about the history of Roman Catholic theology, I believe I am right in saying that it too contains attempts to soften the rigidity of Aquinas' logic. The name of the Jesuit theologian Molina comes to mind in this connection.

Oddly enough it was Luther's close friend and disciple, Philip Melanchthon, who weakened Luther's case. Melanchthon's own position was a form of what is called "synergism," that is that God and man cooperate in the work of salvation. But if you will examine the Lutheran confessions you will see that they do not include Melanchthon's synergistic views and are still on the predestinarian side.

In Calvinism (about fifty years after Calvin's death) the opposition to predestination was centered in a group in the Netherlands called Arminians. But the Arminians were not Pelagians. I mean they never held the position that man of his own free will was capable of choosing and working out his own salvation. I admit that when you listen to some modern evangelists you would think that that was the case. But that would be a very debased form of Arminianism which no thoughtful Arminian would have touched with a ten-foot pole.

No, like the Semi-Pelagians or the Molinists or Melanchthon the Arminians were anxious to find some formula which would preserve what they thought was the best of both predestination and free will. They thought they had such a formula, but it was rejected at the Synod of Dort in 1619.

The point which I wish to make out of all this history is that with the exception of Pelagius nobody has ever contended that every man is free to decide his own religious destiny. All of the opponents of the doctrine of predestination from Semi-Pelagians to Arminians have acknowledged that there was something to it, something which they were anxious to preserve. They only wished to round it off, so to speak, by adding some factors from the other side.

The church has almost always rejected these attempts, though there are some denominations which claim to be officially Arminian in their point of view. But let's not get sidetracked. If almost all of the principal opponents of predestination have agreed that there was much in the doctrine which they too wished to preserve and make more palatable, it would seem to me that here is an even greater argument against throwing it out without a second look. After all, the proponents of the doctrine and the opponents who have wanted to change it only a little bit together make up perhaps ninety per cent of historic Christendom. Or isn't that cloud of witnesses enough for you?

Sincerely,

3

DEAR JAN,

I can see that Pelagius interests you; so let's talk about him in this letter. I think I know why you are so willing to take up the cudgels in his lost cause. A celebrated theologian of our own time is supposed to have said, "Scratch an American and you will find a Pelagian." We Americans are so accustomed to the idea of free will in every field, the notion that what we have we get for ourselves, that we see no reason why it should not be true in the field of religion as well. So condemnation or no, we think we see a kindred spirit in Pelagius.

And to be truthful, there is much in our American Christianity that is Pelagian, whether it would recognize the label or not. When the evangelist exhorts us to accept Jesus as our personal Savior, when the Sunday school teacher pressures us to be good little boys and girls, or when the preacher tells us that the choice is up to us, all of them, know it or not, are good Pelagians, whatever may be their denominational handle.

For, as nearly as we can make out, this is what Pelagius had to say. Every man is completely free to choose salvation or damnation, as free as Adam was in Eden. God has sent Christ into the world that by his teaching and example he might stimulate us into choosing salvation. But that is, so to speak, the limit of God's action. The rest is up to us to whom God has given absolute power of choice.

I may not have done Pelagius justice, but I think I have. And surely you recognize his case. Change Christ's "teaching and example" (Pelagius was really a liberal long before the idea had been thought of) to his "atoning death on Calvary" and you will have the familiar American theme, orthodox or liberal.

But now what is so wrong with the Pelagian point of view? Let me suggest at least three basic objections.

a) There is first of all the psychological objection that the kind of free will which Pelagius talks about is pure myth. It may exist on paper, but it does not exist in real life. Each of us is differently conditioned by environment, to go no further, so that some wills are freer than others. Face to face with the gospel, whether described in Pelagius' terms or some others, my situation may impel me one way while yours moves you in another. If salvation is entirely up to us, then plainly the saved will be only those whose wills have been best conditioned.

b) But the theological (and I may say biblical) objections are still more important. If it is my free choice that saves me, then you cannot deny that I am saved by my own good works. My choosing to believe is just as much a good work as my making a novena or going on a pilgrimage. But this is to land us right back in the very dilemma from which the Reformation tried to deliver us. Let Pelagius have his way and we must always be checking up on ourselves, testing our choices, taking our spiritual temperatures and pulses—in short, we have exposed ourselves to all of that fussy anxiety and uncertainty which Luther knew before his deliverance.

c) I can summarize the final objection by saying quite simply that if Pelagius is right, then there is no such thing as grace. Yes, God sent Christ to do thus and so. But the gospel says that our entire deliverance from start to finish is the work of God's love in action, a work of grace. It is not only a question of what God did in the life, death, and rising again of his Son. It is also a question of what he does by the gift of his Spirit in our minds and hearts. To limit God's grace to the life and teaching of Christ, suggesting that having done that, he now sits and waits for us to respond is to make a terrible caricature of the God of the gospel.

Forget that you ever heard of predestination for the moment. How do you square Pelagianism with the parable of the lost sheep or the lost coin? Can you possibly make a Pelagian out of the author of Psalm 139? Or how would Pelagius account for St. Paul? We may be a long way from a doctrine of predestination. But any theory which fails to take account of both biblical witness and Christian experience must be rejected. And both Bible and experience say that God never waits for our decisions but is at the very least seeking to shape and influence our decisions, that while we, in our self-importance, are trying to make up our minds about him, he has already made up his mind about us. Not only the gospel is grace; our response to it must be grace as well.

Forgive me for sounding like a preacher. But I want you to see why Pelagius will not do. What will do we still have to discuss. But I hope you agree that nothing will suffice which does not begin with the divine initiative.

Sincerely,

4

DEAR JAN,

Well, I am glad to learn that you are no longer a Pelagian, even if you are not yet ready to accept predestination. Mind you, I'm still going to work on you! But even though you have not mentioned it in your correspondence, I should like to use this letter to clear up a common misunderstanding of the idea of predestination which may just be lurking in the back of your mind too.

A good many people whom I know, at any rate, think that by predestination we mean that the entire script for the drama of our lives was written by God before the world began. All we do is repeat the part which has been written for us. Not only the time and place of our birth and death, but everything in between, including the name of the girl we married and the job we have—God is responsible for the whole business. He worked it out in eternity.

When I was in college that idea would have been laughed at. I have the feeling, however, that it has begun to fascinate people again in our time. After all, we live in a world of such chance and change that it's comforting to think that somebody knows what he's doing. When people die of cancer in the prime of life or are killed in an automobile accident while they are still young, it helps to believe that it was not just a senseless happenstance, but part of a plan.

Just because we are no longer so self-confident, just because we are terrified by the prospect of events that have no author, we find ourselves taking another look at this old idea that everything is planned. You hear it when the soldier says, "The only bullet that can kill me is the one that has my number on it." You get it in the common saying, "No one dies before his time." In spite of all our boasts about freedom, we Americans find the idea of a planned existence more congenial than we used to.

I suppose there are biblical and even Christian aspects to this idea. If we were discussing what we mean by the providence of God, we should touch on some of them. But nothing like this is what the Bible or the church has understood by predestination. In fact, this idea, which is usually called *fatalism,* can be found in just about every race and religion. Not even the most orthodox Calvinist has ever suggested that he believed that God and not you is responsible for the fact that you had orange juice for breakfast or that you lost a filling eating mince pie on Thursday. When we Christians speak of predestination we are talking about something quite different.

In fact, it is so different that there is another word for it, *election.* God makes choices and decisions too. He chooses us. Our relationship to him is not the result of our choice of him but of his choice of us. The Bible even asserts that his choice of us is not something which he made after we were born, but something which he determined "before the foundation of the world." The fact that you are a Christian was God's choice, a choice that he made "in the beginning."

There, in briefest and baldest terms, is the thing we shall be talking about, the thing that Augustine, Aquinas, Luther, Zwingli, and Calvin were talking about. Naturally it leads to all kinds of other questions. Does our response have absolutely nothing to do with the case? How about those who reject God's grace? Did God choose them for destruction in the same way that he chose us for salvation? Is damnation as well as redemption a matter of God's election?

I think you will agree that this is a large enough area for our discussion. But I wanted to limit the area before we began. We could do a lot of speculating about the other kind of question. Philosophers have and will doubtless continue to do so. But that is all we could do— speculate. The Bible offers no clear answer. So if by predestination you mean what I have called fatalism, you are going to be disappointed; we shall not be discussing it. But if you mean what I have called election, then in my next letter I am ready to get to work.

But I want to begin where the Bible begins—at the center. And the center is our relationship to God in Jesus Christ. To what extent is that God's deed? And to what extent is it ours?

Sincerely,

5

Dear Jan,

I gather from your reply that you have no objection to our proceeding in the direction which I outlined. Of course, I agree with you. There is much more to be said about God's providence than mere speculation. But you must agree that it is really another topic which we shall have to reserve to a later date.

I want to try a rather dangerous experiment in this letter. I want to omit the Bible for the time being and concentrate instead on what I might call experience. I want to ask you to think carefully about your relationship to Jesus Christ and then ask yourself whether the four things I am about to write are, in your judgment, true.

a) Without Jesus Christ your life would be a mess. I don't mean that you would be a jailbird or sitting in death row, though I seem to recall that Cardinal Newman thought that that was a possibility. I mean that your whole attitude toward life would be different. Your chief interest would be in yourself, and that in the lowest and meanest sense. You would regard other people either as threats to your desires or as means to further them.

Probably you would do a number of things that would be good, so far as anyone could tell. But you would know that what had prompted you, even to friendship and love, was your own self-interest. That taint would be upon everything, even when you tried to be rid of it. Could we go a step further and say that apart from Jesus Christ even your religion would have the taint on it? You would be anxious to please God because in one way or another he could be useful to you. And when he didn't come through, you would either be angry at him, angry enough perhaps to say that he didn't exist, or you would try to coax him into some kind of cooperation.

b) But you do have a living relationship to Jesus Christ. And when you try to analyze how you came by it, you really can claim no credit for it, can you? Never mind now how you came by it in point of fact. We should all have to answer that question differently. But differently as we should answer it, all of our answers would agree in this: we did nothing to deserve this. Even if there is a definite point in our lives at which we said "Yes" to the claims of Christ, we could not claim very much credit for that affirmative response.

c) In fact, if we are honest with ourselves, we should probably admit that we should have preferred to say "No." Just look at the way in which the world thinks about us Christians—the endless trouble we have chosen for ourselves, the ridiculously difficult way of life to which we have committed ourselves, the pain and torment in which we have involved ourselves. Who in his right mind would have taken all this on himself?

Indeed, we can ask the question—would we ever have taken it upon ourselves? If you reply that in your case you had no choice since you inherited it, I can answer that when you were old enough to realize what was involved, you could easily have gotten out. But you didn't, even though I dare say that many times, if you are honest with me, you have wanted to.

d) And that really brings me to the final thing I have to say. Would you not admit that while there have been many times that you wanted out, not to mention the many times (known, of course, only to you) when in terms of your response you deserved to be put out, you are still in. If this relationship to Christ depended entirely upon you and me for its continuance, it would probably have come to an end many times. But it has not. Despite all of our waverings and hesitations, despite all of the many times that we have betrayed the relationship, it is still real. You have read, I am sure, Father Tyrrell's famous line about "the strange man on his cross who drives one back again and again." Well, have you not found it so? Have you not discovered that it is true of the gospel, that those who neither wanted it nor willed it are still attracted to it?

Never mind trying to guess what ulterior motives I may have in mind. Just tell me whether or not the things which I have tried to describe, rather badly I admit, find any echo in your own experience. Then we can go on from there.

Sincerely,

6

DEAR JAN,

From your reply I gather that with the first three of my propositions you have no real trouble. The last one seems to make you hesitate, though you do seem to have some trouble with the third one also. Well, save your objections till we have thought about these propositions in greater detail, as I am sure we shall have done before this correspondence is finished.

My only interest right now is in the fact that what I wrote in my last letter did not strike you as complete nonsense. The important thing is that it did find at least some echoes in your own experience. Don't you see, since that is true you cannot dismiss the idea of election and predestination as silly or the outmoded relic of another day. No longer are you in a position to ask, as you did in your first letter, how seriously we have to take these statements. You have already indicated that to a degree at least you do take them seriously.

Perhaps I have not been playing fair with you. In these four statements I asked you to evaluate I have actually been summarizing and paraphrasing a classic theological statement of the doctrine. These four propositions which you have been thinking over are all part of a full exposition of election and predestination as it was once worked out in the history of theology. The four even have technical names: "total depravity," "unconditional election," "irresistible grace," and "the perseverance of the saints."

Don't worry! I don't intend to make any extensive use of those terms. In fact, I don't think they are very helpful except possibly to the technical theologian. For most people they can even be misleading. No one can possibly cram into three or four words a whole range of ideas and experience. And if you do not know the history of these terms, they can easily throw you.

For example, take the phrase "total depravity." If you knew nothing of its technical meaning and took the phrase as it stands, you would assume it to mean that all of us should be locked up in jail since we are incapable of even one truthful statement or one honest deed. And such an assertion is so obviously contrary to even elementary experience that you would conclude that whoever advanced the idea in the first place was either silly or perverted. But even from the little explanation which I tried to give in my last letter you can see that that is not at all what the phrase means. Since the other three classic phrases are equally susceptible of misinterpretation, I think you can see why I am not going to make use of them.

With your permission I am going to skip over all of the history of the doctrine as well as its classic expositors. The battles of Jansenist and Molinist in France or of Remonstrant and Contra-Remonstrant in Holland are doubtless of great interest to the church historian. And certainly their results are things which we cannot ignore. But I have the feeling that we can easily get lost in the thicket of theological detail and miss the real point. The same thing is true of individual discussions of the question by men like Augustine, Aquinas, Calvin, or even Jonathan Edwards (who, by the way, is not easy reading). I hope that some of our correspondence may stimulate you to read what they had to say. But we shall not be spending much time with any one of them.

No, if it meets with your approval, I should like to use

the next several letters to go into each of the points which I have outlined in somewhat greater detail. I shall want your comments on each one, of course. I do not expect to be able to answer all of your questions or objections. But using these classic propositions as starting points, I hope to show you what the Christian tradition is after when it insists upon the reality of election and predestination as central to its faith.

Sincerely,

7

DEAR JAN,

I sometimes think that our time is one of the easiest in which to believe in the reality of human evil. I am not that much older than you, but even in my younger days it was still fashionable to believe that evil (we never used the word "sin") represented nothing but a temporary aberration which education, slum clearance, and economic prosperity could cure. The essential decency, not to say nobility, of human nature was one of our basic articles of faith.

Well, if he did nothing else, Hitler changed all that! There are pockets of it left here and there, I suppose, but they sound as dated as Longfellow's poetry. In our day, the pendulum has swung to the opposite side. Think of our literary figures, the plays of Tennessee Williams or a novel like Katherine Anne Porter's *Ship of Fools*. Almost to the point of irritation they remind us that human nature is selfish and debased. In fact, I think that the character of Pinky in Graham Greene's novel *Brighton Rock* is a far more eloquent illustration of wickedness than any theologian or preacher could devise. Or with your penchant for literary fashions, I am sure you have read *Lord of the Flies*. Well, what happens to the old theory of the essential innocence and purity of human nature under such an inspection?

No, the preachers and the theologians can keep still. They don't have to say a thing. The poets, the novelists, the dramatists are all saying it for them. They do not say it in theological or biblical language. But you cannot deny that what they are saying is that the human heart is desperately wicked, that man is essentially a snarling, selfish, savage beast. I don't suppose many of them are familiar with the classic discussions and definitions of the matter within the church, but "total depravity" is certainly the heart of their message.

But now you want to interrupt. You want to remind me that Greene and Golding and Williams and Porter are dealing with only one side of human nature. You feel that while the seamy, bestial side of us is being emphasized now more than before, it is largely because contemporary authors tend to exclude normal people from their cast altogether. They have no place for the countless decent ordinary people who quietly go about their business.

Granted, but at that point the psychiatrist steps in to ask who these decent and normal people are. He asks whether we have any awareness of the dark chambers of horror that are hidden behind the facades of normal decency. He wonders whether we have any idea of the tangled motives, the strange and ambiguous ideas that lie behind the lives of people who quietly go about their business.

Well, I have some acquaintance with what the psychiatrist is talking about because my job as a pastor requires that I get behind the facade. It was all symbolized for me once when I had to close out the estate of an elderly gentleman who had died suddenly. The man never missed a service in the church, and from the standpoint of his own devout convictions had often questioned my theology. Yet when I went to his apartment to examine his papers I discovered in a locked cabinet one of the most complete collections of pornography I had ever seen!

An extreme case? Only because in acquiring that

library he acted out some of the dark motives which are there below the surface in all of us. It is not that there is no goodness and decency and nobility in human nature. Given all that we know, there is an extraordinary amount of it. But unless we are living in some kind of dream world in which we refuse reality, we know how the shadow always falls across it. We can see it in the professionally righteous, those whose virtue is so obviously self-centered that it is both amusing and irritating. But can we not also see it in ourselves, and shudder at the calculation which lies behind our generosity, the caution which is hidden beneath our goodness?

I really have had no other point in this letter other than to say that the Christian tradition is just as realistic about human nature as Karl Marx or Sigmund Freud. I know that a lot of people have tried to sentimentalize that tradition into cheery bits about the divinity of human personality. Pay no attention to them; they are heretics. No matter the contemporary terms into which you translate it, "total depravity" is the Christian witness to human nature. No Williams or Sartre could put the case for the meaninglessness or hopelessness of human existence more completely than the Bible: "Wretched man that I am! Who will deliver me?"

And on that hopeless note, I shall leave you.

Sincerely,

8

Dear Jan,

Of course, you are right! I exaggerated the hopelessness of the human situation in my last letter because I left God out of it. And certainly, as you point out, the gospel never leaves God out of it; he has been in it from the very beginning. So that I agree with you that any attempt to depict the human situation without God is a false one. But you must admit that for purposes of analysis I had to do it.

Incidentally, let me digress here just long enough to say that this is the basis of my objection to the description of human nature by our modern dramatists and novelists. They picture sin without grace, if I may put it theologically. But that has never been the case since the days of Adam. God has always been involving himself in the hopelessness of our human situation.

But that leads me to the very question I want to take up next. *How* has he involved himself? I do not mean *in what ways:* the Bible is the record of that. No, I mean *on what basis.* I raise the question because there has always been an attempt to smuggle human merit into the picture here by replying that God intervenes in assistance of some good which he sees in human nature. In other words, there is some good in some men which elicits the gracious favor of God's help.

But can't you see that if the description of human nature which I made in my last letter is true, such an answer is silly? What really good thing is there in human nature which could elicit God's help? What is so significant in the behavior of that decent, normal man that it could compel God's assistance? If we take God and his moral character seriously, we have to answer, "Nothing."

Another parenthesis, if you will allow it. I sometimes think that one of the reasons why our hopeless modern authors are so hopeless is that they think of the Christian gospel in terms of the old Pelagian "God helps those who help themselves" thesis. And because they are honest they realize that there is nothing in human existence worth helping. The idea of something in human nature that could elicit the divine assistance is just too ridiculous to consider. So they turn away from the possibility of grace.

But, if I may say so, grace is possible just because it is impossible! It is grace just because there is nothing in the human situation that warrants it. At least that's true of the God of the gospel. God's choice to redeem man is, in the traditional phrase, "unconditioned." There is nothing in our situation that compels him to do anything. He acts not because we deserve it, but purely from love. That's what we mean by "grace."

I hope you will not think that I am insisting upon some kind of theological technicality if I stress the importance of this point. Please do not think that I am in some way trying to defend God's honor by maintaining that the initiative in our redemption is entirely his. I am sure he wouldn't particularly care about that one way or another, just so long as we are redeemed!

No, my insistence comes from quite a different direction. You see, if there is something, however slight, that we can do to compel God's help, we have landed ourselves in the realm of magic. It is a popular Protestant trick to sneer at the Roman Catholic manipulation of God through the Sacrament and make disparaging remarks about the mass as magic. Well, it seems to me that such sneers come with very poor grace when we Protestants are often guilty of a kind of "moral magic." By that I mean that we take the line that by doing certain things, living by a certain standard, refraining from certain actions, we can win God's assistance. It comes perilously close to saying, "He'll have to help me after all I have done for him."

But even more important than this, I think, is the fact that if we condition God's grace in any way we really open the way to the terrible sin of pride. Wasn't this exactly what happened to the Pharisees? They were convinced that God's love was conditioned by all of their legal niceties with the result that their pride became their damnation. Their story has been repeated too often in subsequent Protestant history not to give us considerable pause. Give us even a toehold and we human beings will begin to tell God how to run his business; that seems to be the moral of the story.

I realize that I have raised many new questions, not the least of which is, "If what you say is true, why bother to be good?" We still have to consider also who it is that God has chosen to help, just certain people or everybody. But will you admit that in insisting on the unconditioned character of God's choice we are contending for something terribly important?

Sincerely,

9

Dear Jan,

I remember as I start to write this letter that this point was one of those to which you had some objection when I first mentioned it. "Irresistible grace" carries with it the suggestion that you are a Christian in spite of yourself. And, as I recall, you didn't like that too well.

Well, I could reply by asking whether you really think that you are a Christian because of yourself. I am not now referring to the fact that you were born into a Christian home, surrounded during your childhood by Christian influences, and subject to a rather large amount of Christian pressure by your parents. I should be glad to argue, if I had to, that all of these things were part of God's grace, but I do not think that it is in them that its irresistibility comes most sharply into focus.

What I am referring to is our conscious acceptance of this faith as our own. I'm not now interested in how that came to you, whether as the result of a crisis or of a long slow development. What I am interested in is knowing whether you can really say it was something you did. (I don't expect you to answer to me; I only want you to answer to yourself.)

Whatever your answer to the question may be, I think you will find that the answer of those who have entered most deeply into the meaning of this gospel has always been not only to disclaim any credit for their choice but to admit that their own choice would probably have been quite different. An emotional teenager may say jubilantly,

"I chose Jesus." But a little experience will inform him how superficial that remark is.

The saints have always known (and this has been their deepest joy) that God chose them. Sometimes he had quite a battle to make his choice stick. You will know what I mean if you know anything about the biography of a man like Augustine or John Donne or Gerard Manley Hopkins. Sometimes, so far as we can tell, the choice met with little resistance. But I suspect that often what strikes us as effortless and easy really represents, if the facts were fully known, a long and arduous search on God's part.

An anonymous hymn writer once put it in this way:

> I sought the Lord, and afterward I knew
> He moved my soul to seek him, seeking me;
> It was not I that found, O Saviour true;
> No, I was found of thee.

That, very simply, is the only point that I am trying to make. In the heat and press of the moment we may think indeed that the decision was ours. Everything in the picture may serve to convince us that it was ours. God rather enjoys anonymity. But when we begin to reflect upon it and actually trace out the motives, the variety of possibilities, we begin to see that it was not our doing at all. God was at work in our lives, though we did not know it. What we had imagined was our choice was really his grace.

Even though several hundred miles separate us, I can see you scratching your head because you have an important question to ask. "If God's grace is really irresistible," you are going to say, "then how come so many people are apparently resisting it? Do you want to force me into an admission that he offers it to some and withholds it from others? If that's your game, I'm not ready to make any such admission at all."

I don't want to shunt your question aside. It is one with which we must wrestle before we are finished. And I will frankly admit that it is just about the most difficult one that can be asked. But will you understand me if at the moment I say that it is irrelevant?

I have always liked that little episode which comes at the end of John's Gospel. Do you remember how Peter pointed to John and asked Jesus, "Lord, what about this man?" "What is that to thee?" replied our Lord, "Follow thou me." Well, I don't want to seem pious. But at this moment we are not ready to begin asking questions about other people. I can't even ask them about you. I can only ask and answer them about *this man*. And *this man* is willing to admit that through all the tortured web of his existence, the proud decisions, the shrinking failures, the victories and the defeats, he can trace the irresistible hand of Christ. The only thing that makes him different from those wretched creatures in a Tennessee Williams' play is grace—and that not of his choosing but of God's giving.

Sincerely,

10

DEAR JAN,

I gather from your last letter that, while you have some reservations along the way, you are going to hold them back until I have finished my presentation and then spring them on me. Good! I had the impression that you were assenting much too easily. But let me say that I approve of your waiting not simply because it makes my task easier for the moment but because these four ideas I have been setting forth are not separate items, each one standing by itself, but parts of an entire design. I think it is a good thing for you to see the whole picture before you pass judgment on it.

So let's turn to the fourth and last proposition which is traditionally called "the perseverance of the saints." Some wiseacre once remarked that it would be more realistic to talk about the "perseverance of the sinners." And from a human point of view, it really would, you know. When you consider the ways in which the world sticks to the job it wants to get done until it gets it done, and compare that persistence with the feeble, halfhearted way in which the saints go about the business of the kingdom, there can be no doubt where the prize for perseverance would have to go. If the world ran its business the way the saints run the church, we should have had economic disaster long ago.

I'm not just kidding. Our parish is in a large city. You have been interested in our attempts to make a dent in some of the less happy parts of that city which are fairly near our front door. Well, when you compare the perseverance of the dopepushers, the numbers racketeers, the saloon keepers and the streetwalkers with ours, it's pretty discouraging.

But of course, that's not what the traditional phrase is talking about. Or is it? To be sure, it is not talking about human perseverance. That's not worth talking about, unless it happens to be in a bad cause. Then, apparently, it can be very dedicated indeed! The phrase is talking about God's perseverance. And it seems to me to be saying at least two things.

For one thing, it is saying that since my relationship to Jesus Christ is God's choice and not mine, nothing I can do can foul it up. Even when I betray him, he is there still asking, "Do you love me?" still saying, "Feed my sheep." People have interpreted this as an invitation to license. If it be true, they say, then we can do anything we please and not worry about the consequences. Such people don't know what they are talking about.

In actual fact the effect has always been quite different. It has been one of encouragement and renewal. Any man who takes the gospel seriously knows that if his mistakes could ruin his relationship to Christ, it would have been ruined soon after it began. After all, the gospel is not *Poor Richard's Almanac,* the provisions of which could be kept by any well-intentioned citizen. It is the gospel of the cross, the cross which we too must shoulder. And who of us is up to that? Denial and betrayal come mighty easily when the cross is the only other alternative.

But these failures cannot deprive God of what he has chosen. With mercy and forgiveness, he waits to claim us again. An old Scottish preacher once said, "The perseverance of the saints is made up of ever new beginnings." And that is just the glory of it, that in Christ there can be ever new beginnings, even from the most shameful failures.

But in the second place I think this phrase has something to say to the "perseverance of the sinners" which I mentioned earlier in this letter. When we compare the strength of the church with the strength of the world which it is to win for Christ, we find it pretty discouraging. What are our pennies compared with their millions? What are our sporadic efforts compared with their intense zeal?

Well, the perseverance of the saints means that God is not on the side of the biggest budgets but on the side of Jesus Christ. It may seem the prudential thing to give up, to go along. But the gospel is never prudential. We may not know how the slums of a city can be conquered by Christ. But God knows. He has made his choice and his choices stick!

What I am really saying is that this old doctrine of the perseverance of the saints is the only basis we have for the mission of the church. Without it, we can do social service, give medical assistance, render psychological aid. But with it, and only with it, can we move in to conquer.

Sincerely,

11

Dear Jan,

Please don't be upset by your dilemma. It is just the result that I had hoped for. If I get your point correctly, you are disturbed by the fact that your experience tends to confirm everything that I have been saying about pre-destination and election, but that when you try to make a logical case of it, you are in a terrible mess. Fine! You have made the exact point that I wanted you to make.

Don't you see, election is exactly like all the great doctrines of the faith. They did not come into being because the apostles enjoyed spinning theological theories. They came into being because men had to confess what had happened to them. I think the doctrine of the Trinity provides something of a parallel. Not one of the early Christians was at all interested in how three could be one or one three. But every one of them knew that he could not describe the full reality of his new life unless he said "Father, Son, and Holy Spirit."

Similarly with election. All of our debates about conditioned or unconditioned election, foreordination, and what have you would probably have puzzled a New Testament Christian no end. All that he knew was that if it was to describe the full dimension of his new life in Christ he had to say that everything was of God and nothing was his own doing.

In fact, this is always true of the New Testament. It does not deal in doctrines. It records the raw facts of experience, out of which doctrine can be constructed.

Perhaps I should have gone into what the New Testament has to say about our subject before this. I certainly intend to before we have finished. But I thought it might be better first to see what the experience behind this difficult doctrine is in terms which we can match from our own experience.

I thought you might be interested in a confirmation of this experience not from one of the great saints but from an ordinary layman. James Anthony Froude, the nineteenth-century British historian, was, if you know anything about him, neither pious nor orthodox. In fact, he pretty much belonged to the left wing of Anglicanism. But here is what he wrote to his friend Charles Kingsley.

> I and you alike agree that man is what the grace of God makes him. We did not make ourselves. We have never overcome our evil inclination without God's grace given us as a free gift. Neither is it any act of our own will, further than that will is itself the power of God working in us which enables us to receive grace. Place for what is called *free will* as something of our own independent of God there is none in human nature, and God forbid that there should be. If I thought there was I should be a Catholic or an atheist tomorrow.*

Well, there is the experience. Did you ever hear Dr. Johnson's bon mot about predestination? "All logic is for it," he said, "and all experience against it." I hesitate to disagree with the great lexicographer, but I must say that I think exactly the reverse is the truth. All experience is for it and all logic against it. Just as you said in your letter, so long as we stay with the realities of our own Christian experience election provides no difficulty. It is when we try to make a logical presentation of it that the brain staggers and the reason reels.

* Waldo H. Dunn, *James Anthony Froude, A Biography, 1818-1856* (Oxford: Clarendon Press, 1961), p. 191.

That leads me to make two observations. First, if we stop to think about it, whenever we try to reduce God and his mighty acts to the statements of human logic we are going to be in trouble. How could it be otherwise? To express infinity in finite terms is manifestly impossible. There must always be gaps and difficulties. I do not want to sound captious, but I sometimes wish that some of the fathers who expounded the doctrine could have remembered that. They made the case too easy, too neat. Even though their hearts were certainly in the right place, I often feel that they tried to prove too much. So don't expect a neat logical package from me!

The other thing I want to say is this: it is patently silly to try to explain predestination to someone who does not stand within the experience. It is so much religious algebra to him and nothing more. But once he stands within the experience of redemption, the algebra comes alive and begins to glow with meaning. The experience, in short, must precede the logic.

But the logic has to be there too. After all, we live in a world in which we must try to communicate our experience—that's how doctrine is born. So now that we have more or less established the experience, let's have a go at the logic by seeing what some of the kinks in it are. Which one would you like to try to straighten out first?

Sincerely,

DEAR JAN,

So you'd like to begin your objections by defending Dr. Johnson! I gather from your letter that you feel that there is one sense in which he was right. So far as we can tell our choices seem to be our choices. We are not usually aware of any divine pressure or influence. We are aware only of an appeal to which we respond. If this is a true reading of our experience, then do we not have to agree with Sam and say that all experience is against predestination? That's your objection, isn't it?

Well, of course, you are really raising a very basic question about the validity of free will. Is there really such a thing? Or more properly, I suppose, does the doctrine of election leave any place for it? We can easily get lost in this kind of discussion, especially if we let it get moved into the whole business of psychological determinism and all that sort of thing. That I should like to avoid if I can.

But I do think we have to get into it just long enough to point out that the idea (of which I seem to see some traces in your letter) that man is a kind of neutral being who can choose to go this way or that is pure myth. We like to think of ourselves in our moral and religious choices as travelers at a crossroads, trying to decide whether to go to Boston or Providence. And that of course is pure moonshine. In all of these choices we are not neutral beings, but persons who have been subjected to influences and experiences, all of which condition the choice which we make.

I could dwell for quite a while on the fact that both the Bible and the Christian faith insist that in our human situation we are capable only of bad choices. In fact, if we take the idea of "total depravity" seriously, to what other conclusion could we come? You recall what our Lord once said, "Every one who commits sin is a slave to sin." That is to say, however we may see fit to choose, as unredeemed human beings we can only choose wrong.

But to come back to the question which you have raised. Since the choices which we make are the results of all kinds of influences at work in our personalities, is it so difficult to believe that the grace of God is one of those influences? You write almost as if you believed that when God influences our choices he does it with letters of fire in the sky, or some dramatic means which make it clear that it is his choice and not ours.

But you don't really believe that. Grace never comes in that way. I could, of course, refer you to Elijah's experience with the "still, small voice." But I like Jonathan Edwards' phrase better. No one, I suppose, was a more skilled student of grace. Do you know how he defined it? "A new idea in the mind." The description may be overly intellectual, but I think it is very profound. That new idea in the mind, which is the grace of God's good Spirit, is ours. Yet it never could have been ours had it not been for God. His election is accomplished not by the annihilation of our will, but by the redemption of our will through his grace.

I found an excellent description of what I am trying to say in (of all places) the writings of Ralph Waldo Emerson. In speaking of religion he wrote:

> It is not something else to be got, to be added, but is a new life of those faculties you have. It is to do right; it is to love; it is to serve; it is to think; it is to be humble.

I make no claim to understand Emerson's theology! Nor do I know in just what sense he meant those words, since I found them out of context. But make *grace* the antecedent of the opening pronoun and Emerson is merely amplifying Edwards. God's grace is not some shattering experience that compels us to say "Yes" because we are too overawed to say anything else. It is the reanimation and redirection of our whole personality, a personality we have wasted and even destroyed by years of misuse.

Mind you, I do not want anything I have written to be interpreted as saying that in some way we cooperate with God in the work of our salvation. That way lies danger. All that I am saying is that God works anonymously. Often it is not until after the decision has been reached, the step has been taken, the road traveled that we are aware of what it really was that brought us to our present situation.

Experience is still a valid argument. But not unless we are willing to examine the full dimensions of what we have experienced!

Sincerely,

13

Dear Jan,

I knew it had to come sooner or later! If our salvation is God's election, can the same thing be said of our damnation? If there are those who reject the good news of the gospel, did God predestine them to their rejection? You really want to get me over a barrel, don't you? If I say "Yes," then, of course, you are going to explode that I am sub-Christian and that my reply makes God an arbitrary despot, a horrible tyrant, in no way resembling the Father of Jesus Christ. And if I say "No," then, obviously, I have thrown the whole case out the window. For I can't have it both ways. So I am caught in a trap.

Well, strangely enough, no less a person than Augustine did try to have it both ways. He tried to say that while God chooses the elect and predestines them to salvation, he simply lets the damned go their own way. He does nothing but let them suffer the consequences of their depravity. But I am sure we both agree that for a number of reasons that is not a very satisfactory solution to the problem.

Calvin, on the other hand, did not shrink from the full logic of the case. He clearly believed in double predestination; just as God has willed some to salvation, so he has willed others to damnation. (Incidentally, you should know that in theological language, the opposite of salvation is *reprobation* in case I should forget myself and use the term.)

His was at least an honest answer to your question,

though an answer, I may say, from which a good many Calvinists both now and in the past have rather shrunk. Calvin felt that double predestination could be defended first of all because there are certain passages in Scripture which seem to support it (more about these later). He also felt that it was defensible because it honored both God's justice and his mercy. The reprobate has no complaint; he is simply receiving the just reward of his wickedness and so God maintains his justice. The elect certainly has no complaint; he is the object of totally unmerited mercy which is also part of God's character.

I certainly don't need to tell you that critics have jumped all over Calvin at this point. And while I have to admit that much of their criticism seems to me justified, I have had an increasing sympathy with poor old John. Perhaps he was the victim of his own logic. But at least he did something which many of his critics have never done. He took evil seriously. He didn't try to sentimentalize it. Better than our shallow breed of ecclesiastical optimists, he knew what was in the human heart, knew the terrible mystery of evil. Perhaps his theory was the result of too much logic. But I have a sneaking suspicion that it was reinforced at least in his pastoral experience. It is a terrible thing to meet someone (I have had it happen only once or twice) who has descended the spiral stairway so far that he no longer knows he is going down, let alone has any desire to find his way back up. Perhaps we of the twentieth century are in a better position to understand Calvin's grimness than were his nineteenth century critics. How do you suppose they would have accounted for Hitler?

But even so, I recognize the difficulties in Calvin's case. For one thing, his division of justice and mercy in the divine character is fatally wrong. God is not just every Tuesday and merciful every Friday, as it were.

He cannot be merciful without being just any more than he can be just without being merciful. A Scottish minister is reported to have said, "God must do some things in his official capacity which he would rather not do personally!" We cannot have the integrity of God's moral character broken up in that way.

But I think an even more telling criticism of Calvin is to be found in the fact that his discussion of this question is carried on almost completely without reference to Jesus Christ. This is strange because Calvin was a keen student of Scripture. And the New Testament discussion is always centered in the fact that we were "chosen in Christ" before the foundation of the world. I am not saying that if Calvin had paid more heed to this he would have come out differently. But I do say that his discussion would have been more biblical and much less metaphysical.

Well, I have not really answered your question, have I? I have only tried in this letter to give it a little historical perspective. I'm not even sure I'll get to it in my next letter for there is still some ground to be cleared.

Sincerely,

14

DEAR JAN,

I think my real objection to Calvin's double pre-destination is the non-biblical way in which he carries on the discussion. I do not mean that he does not buttress his case with many scriptural allusions. I mean that it is a piece of theological logic. Since we have established that all things depend upon the will of God and since we can see that certain people reject the grace of God, we must conclude that their rejection is itself the will of God. I oversimplify, I know, but that's about the way Calvin's thought goes.

Perhaps it will do as a piece of theological logic. But logic ought not to intrude in a realm where it really has no competence. That's the first thing that must be said. I know of a no more sincere Calvinist in our time than the late Professor Auguste Lecerf of Paris. But I think his words are significant:

> Predestination implies in fact a meeting of eternity and time. The very word *pre*destination, with the pre-fix *pre* attached to the word destination, presupposes a sense of an eternal act, one which is therefore unchange-ably present, considered from the point of view of time, of a before and after. Furthermore, since predestina-tion involves a relationship between God and his creatures, we are involved in a meeting of the Infinite with the finite. All of this warns our finite reason, when it wants to be reasonable, that it is in the midst of a mystery which it cannot fathom. If our reason does not discover insoluble contradictions in the problem, that is a sign that it is mistaken, that it has omitted some element of the truth.*

* A. Lecerf, *Etudes Calvinistes* (Neuchâtel: Delachaux et Niestlé, 1949), p. 28.

But, at the risk of sounding repetitious, let me point out again that the Bible never broaches this question about other people. It always puts the question bluntly to us. And, even though I may not seem to be answering your question very directly, that is where I should like to begin. The elect know who they are. They know it, I may say, without pride, but they know it confidently and gratefully. Perhaps you have read some of those terrible spiritual diaries from Puritan New England in which young people lay awake in terror all night wondering if they were damned. Well, that is not good New Testament Christianity. Whoever knows Jesus Christ belongs to the elect. May I quote Professor Lecerf again?

> It is not up to you to ask by whatever means you can whether you belong to the elect. It is up to you to believe the gospel, and then, because you have believed, you can read on the cross of Christ the liberating decree: "He who believes in me," Christ said, "has eternal life and nothing shall snatch him out of my hand."*

That is all we really can know or need to know—our own situation with regard to Jesus Christ.

But then let me try to establish a second point. The elect do not know who the reprobate are. How could they? This is something which is known only to God. To try to make his decisions and judgments for him is to fall into Adam's sin all over again. Thus, if I may say so, it is not up to us to speculate about the fate of those who have never heard the gospel or to assign them a place among the damned. Our job is to see that the gospel is preached to them, and to leave the rest of God's mercy which we can certainly trust because we have known it ourselves. Similarly, it is not our responsibility to pass judgment upon our neighbors. Our task again is simply to bring the good news to them.

* *Ibid.*, p. 29.

I wonder whether I am entitled to make a third point. It may sound strange but I should like to advance the thesis that the reprobate do not know who they are. They could know that really only if they know Jesus Christ. But if a man really knows Jesus Christ, how can he be damned? It is, for example, not even said of Judas with certainty in the Scriptures that he was finally condemned.

It may seem to you that I have been saying in a roundabout way that there is no such thing as a damned person. I have not, although there are those who have drawn that conclusion. Universalism has been spooking around Christian circles for at least 1,700 years. All that I have been wanting to say is that reprobation is something that lies completely outside our realm of knowledge. No man can stand up and say "I am damned." For to say that implies some knowledge of Jesus Christ and who can say where even that little knowledge may finally bring him? On the other hand, any man who believes in Christ can stand up and say, "I am saved." The only thing we can know for sure is our own election and the responsibilities which that involves. Everything else is theory and speculation.

But if we cannot know a reprobate, can we know what he would look like? If we cannot know who the damned are, can we conceive of the dimensions of damnation? That's a question I should like to take up in my next letter.

Sincerely,

15

DEAR JAN,

Please do not worry about getting lost in this discussion. Better men than you and I have done so! But that does not excuse us from the necessity of facing up to it. I know that in this age of sentimental religion it has become fashionable to dismiss hell and damnation as totally irreconcilable with the love of God—as if the love of God had no moral character, were not holy love. Well, it is a position which is pretty difficult to square with the clear witness both of our Lord and the Scriptures. That is enough for me (and I am sure for you) to require some thinking about it.

At the same time let me hasten to add that I have no sympathy whatever with the crude fundamentalism which knows exactly what hell is, what its temperature is, and can almost list off its inhabitants. That kind of business (which is really just as unfaithful to the New Testament as the other) has done untold harm, I am sure, in frightening people away from any serious consideration of the question.

Let me go back to the question with which I closed my last letter. That question, it seems to me, expresses our real difficulty. If I may add a fourth proposition to the three I made in that letter, it would be this. Only the elect can really know what reprobation could be like. I think that even superficial observation will bear that out. The only people who can imagine the dimensions of damnation are the very people who are not going to experience them because they believe in Christ. The world has no idea about it and couldn't care less. In the world hell is a joke, the devil a clown, and damnation a meaningless term.

But to us who believe, there is nothing funny in all this. Just because we believe, we have some idea of the sheer horror of being without God. We can have it primarily because we have been at the foot of the cross and heard that truly terrifying cry, "My God, my God, why hast thou forsaken me?" And we alone can have it, even as darkness can be described only by those who have experienced light. That is to say, just because we have experienced the love and mercy of God in Christ, we can grasp the possibility, at least, of being without that love and mercy.

And yet just because we know His mercy the possibility of being without it is to us what Karl Barth has called an "impossible possibility." Because we know the lengths to which that love went to find and restore us, we find it impossible to imagine any life which could ultimately elude that love. Because there was nothing in our stubborn pride that was able to block God's mercy and forgiveness, we cannot really see how anything in anyone's life could be able to block it. May I quote from another contemporary churchman who has explored this problem?

> Final unbelief, the cause of reprobation, is indeed an "impossible possibility." How can a man resist God when he knows who He is? How can a man want to resist His grace which is our crowning good? Only an insane person could prefer eternal death to eternal life. He must be possessed by the devil who does not believe when he has received the gift of the Holy Spirit. Our reason cannot conceive of such a possibility; it is the contradiction of all contradictions which reason must reject. And when we meet an unbeliever, we can never

believe that he has committed the sin against the Holy Spirit. We can only believe that God has not yet fully enlightened him.

Reprobation is an "impossible possibility." And yet it is not so impossible that we cannot conceive of it.*

Yes, we can conceive of it—and only we can conceive of it. It is that fact which makes our responsibility to our neighbors so terribly urgent. For reprobation is a present reality. Like the kingdom of heaven, the kingdom of hell is also in the midst of us. For all we know, it may be in our very neighborhood.

I say *for all we know* because, of course, we don't actually know. Only God knows for whom, if anyone, this impossible possibility is a reality. Nor will the revelation of his decision be known until the end of history. To approach our neighbor on the assumption that he is damned is to arrogate to ourselves the right of judgment which belongs alone to God. Only because we who belong to God in Christ have some idea of what a fearful thing it is to fall into the hands of the living God must we testify with the living sacrifice of our total person what a wonderful thing it is to be under his mercy in Christ.

But I still haven't answered your original question, have I? No, but can you see why I have spent these several letters working up to it? I have been trying to give it its full context. Let us assume that it is possible that a man who fully knew the grace of God in Jesus Christ rejected it, finally and completely. This is the only description of damnation that makes any sense. Whose decision was involved in this rejection? God's or his own? I believe that's your question, and we'll look at in the next letter.

Sincerely,

---

* Gaston Deluz, *Prédestination et Liberté* (Neuchâtel: Delachaux et Niestlé, 1942), p. 161.

16

Dear Jan,

Yes, I will stop hedging. If you want to know whether I think that the realization of the impossible possibility of eternal destruction is God's choice for some people, I answer "No." I am fully aware that in taking this position I am opposing some very considerable theological authorities, for all of whom I have great respect.

But I feel that I have to take this position for a number of reasons. While I can understand the logic of double predestination from one point of view (and I want to comment on it before I am through), there is another logic here which seems to me more convincing. If you accept my earlier statement that God's election is accomplished in us by the gracious influence of his Spirit impelling us to choose Christ, then, if we accept the logic of a double predestination, we should have to say that that same Spirit was at work in the reprobate impelling him to choose evil. We should find ourselves in the ludicrous position of saying that the Spirit of God persuades men to commit the sin against the Spirit!

I can appreciate the difficulty. The advocates of double predestination wanted to avoid Augustine's having it both ways. They wanted to preserve the complete integrity of the will of God, leaving room for nothing that could happen apart from that will. If therefore salvation is purely and simply the result of God's holy will, reprobation must be the same.

But here I think, though I say it cautiously, that they would have been better advised to forsake the strong promptings of philosophy and metaphysics and limit themselves to the Bible. To the logician it may seem absurd to say that God chooses some to salvation and simply lets the others perish. But the Scriptures were not written by logicians; they were written by those who could do nothing but testify to their glorious experience of redemption in Jesus Christ.

I have no intention of making up a list of proof-texts to support what I have said. But would you not agree that the whole tenor of the New Testament is to present election and predestination in its positive terms? To begin with, how can we maintain that eternal destruction is the will of God for any man in the light of statements (and they are many) such as that in I Timothy 2:3-4: ". . . God our Savior . . . desires all men to be saved, and to come to the knowledge of the truth." Both the words of our blessed Lord and the writings of Paul are too full of similar statements to allow of any doubt on the point. God's will for every man is salvation in Christ.

But look at the way Paul speaks whenever he speaks of election and predestination. There are again examples too numerous to list here. Let me give you just a couple of samples. "Blessed be the God and Father of our Lord Jesus Christ, who has blessed us in Christ with every spiritual blessing in the heavenly places, even as he chose us in him before the foundation of the world, that we should be holy and blameless before him. He predestined us in love to be his sons through Jesus Christ, according to the purpose of his will" (Eph. 1:3-5). Or what about these words? "For those whom he foreknew, he also predestined to be conformed to the image of his Son, in order that he might be the first-born among many brethren. And those whom he predestined he also called; and those whom he called he also justified; and those whom he justified he also glorified" (Rom. 8:29-30).

Well, I could go on for many more pages piling one text on another to indicate that the clear witness of the New Testament is not only that God's will is salvation, but that whenever election or predestination are spoken of, they are always election and predestination in Christ. It is never said that what has been prepared from before the foundation of the world is man's damnation, but always man's salvation. In the face of such authority, I find it impossible to believe that God is the author of reprobation or that he inclines any to damnation.

It may occur to you to wonder why men who, after all, were keen students of the Scriptures should have missed this. Are there no other passages in the Bible that would support their contention that predestination is double, both to salvation and to damnation? Surely they must have had some biblical sanction for their position.

Of course they did. And I suppose that to be fair we should have a look at those passages. I'll make a bargain with you. If you can find them by your next letter, I'll discuss them!

Sincerely,

17

Dear Jan,

Did you sit up all night with a Bible and a concordance? Well, congratulations anyway, because you certainly put your finger on the principal passage on which the proponents of double predestination have rested their case. There are a few others here and there in the Bible, but Romans 9:13-23 is indeed the chief one. And I think I should point out not only that its words come from the same Paul I was quoting in my last letter, but that they appear only a little later in the same context as those from Romans 8 which I there quoted.

This crucial passage is not easy, as you say. I think we ought to observe in the first place that Paul is not discussing double predestination as such, but the whole question of Israel's rejection of the gospel. I mention that because it is important to keep these words in their context and not try to extend their application into all sorts of directions where Paul, as we know from his other writings, would have been quite unwilling to have them apply. Thus, for example, I have seen the words in verse 13 "Jacob I loved, but Esau I hated" interpreted to mean that God saves some and sends others to hell. But surely that is drawing out the meaning of Paul's quotation of Malachi far beyond his own intention or that of the prophet.

We could, of course, proceed verse by verse. But I think it better to try to make certain general statements. Is it not clearly Paul's purpose in this passage to say what

I have been trying to say all along in this correspondence, namely, that God's mercy is free and nobody can lay claim to it on any basis whatever. This was Israel's fault. Having been chosen by God's mercy, they felt they had God in a box. All they had to do was remind him that they were Abraham's children and he would have to respond. And here is Paul to remind them that neither bloodline nor past performance gives any nation or individual any claim upon the sovereignly free love of God (a healthy reminder for us, by the way, as well as for Israel).

Anyway, if you read on to the end of this section, which closes with the eleventh chapter, you will see how absurd it is to try to use this passage to prove a predestination to damnation. For the same Israel which has for the moment been rejected will, Paul assures us in Romans 11:25-26, finally be saved. "A hardening has come upon part of Israel, until the full number of the Gentiles come in, and so all Israel will be saved." I am not interested now in tracing out the rather tortuous thread of Paul's argument in Romans 9-11. My purpose is simply to point out that it does not strike me as having anything particularly to say to our question of final reprobation.

Verses 9:20-23 are, I admit, rather difficult. Their meaning, as all commentators agree, is obscure. I think that Dr. Dodd is rather ducking the issue when he writes, "When Paul, normally a clear thinker, becomes obscure, it usually means that he is embarrassed by the position he has taken up."* But even taking the words at their face value, Paul never actually says that God creates some vessels for the purpose of destroying them—which would have to be the logic of double predestination. Some, to be sure, are created only for "menial use" (vs. 21). But that

* Quoted in *The Interpreter's Bible* (12 vols.; New York: Abingdon-Cokesbury, 1954), IX, 548.

is to say no more than our Lord himself said in the parable of the talents. God "has endured with much patience the vessels of wrath made for destruction" (vs. 22). But is Paul not saying here essentially the same thing that Jesus said in his parable of the wheat and the tares? We live in the time of God's patience, the time between the gift of the Spirit and the final consummation of history. In that time, God withholds his final judgment. I agree that Paul's language could be pushed further. But it seems to me that pushing it that way in the light of everything else he has said on this subject is unwarranted.

I am well aware that there are still many thorns left in this passage. But I still maintain that those who want to find double predestination here are reading their theory into Paul's words which were, after all, addressed to a very special problem. And since everywhere else the same Paul says that election is election in Christ to salvation, I am willing to rest my case there.

Sincerely,

18

DEAR JAN,

You're not easily satisfied, are you? You still want to pose a dilemma. If there are those who finally reject the grace of God and so are left to the consequences of their depravity, must we not say that this was in God's foreknowledge and therefore part of his predestination? If that is so, are we not still saying, even though at one remove, that God is responsible for human evil since he lets it alone and does nothing to prevent it?

We could have a great time with this question if we wanted to. Oceans of ink and tons of paper have been consumed in the attempt to distinguish between foreknowledge and predestination, the attempt to excuse God from or blame him for the evil that is in human nature. I hope you will understand me when I say that I am not really going to answer your question since I do not think it is a question which we can even ask, much less answer.

For one thing the Scriptures afford us no basis for asking it. Please do not think I am trying to be a narrow biblicist. But I think you will agree that we have no basis for asking any question about God except as he has revealed himself in his Word. Everything else is the kind of guesswork which is absolutely futile.

Now as I have observed before, the only kind of question the Bible authorizes us to ask is a personal question: What is God's relationship to his people? What is his relationship to me? With respect to this kind of question there is every encouragement for both the asking and the answering. But the moment we try to climb the heights of speculation and ask a philosophical question about God's foreknowledge of somebody else whom we do not even know and cannot with any certainty identify, we have absolutely no ground under our feet.

But even apart from biblical considerations, we are really asking a question which it is impossible to ask for purely logical reasons. When you ask whether God by foreknowing those who would choose evil and then letting them do it, is not therefore necessarily responsible for evil, in one sense the answer is "Yes" since obviously God created a world in which evil is possible. But the question comes perilously close to asking whether God could not have made a different world from the one which he did make. And that question obviously makes no sense at all. This is the world which he did make and these are the possibilities for us in it. If we begin to speculate about the kind of worlds God might have made, we are just talking nonsense.

After warning you against philosophy and speculation, it may seem strange to you that I should indulge in it a little myself. But it has always seemed to me that part of our problem with this whole question of foreknowledge and predestination is our inability to think of eternity except in terms of time. If I foreknow, for example, that you are going to attempt to steal my car, I take steps to prevent it. But my knowledge and my subsequent action are separated in time, if only by minutes. And because this is the only kind of experience we have, we find it quite natural to assume that God is similarly bound. Having foreknown certain eventualities, he then decided what to do about them, and finally decreed his intention.

But, of course, to God there is neither past, present, nor future. The end and the beginning, so to speak, are seen in a single glance. For him there is no distinction between knowledge and action. I have always felt the force of Jonathan Edwards' observation that God did not see the sin of Adam and then condemn all his descendants because of it. Because God sees from eternity and not in time, when he saw Adam he saw all mankind.

I am not sure I know just what this proves, except negatively. It certainly is a warning against trying to construct theories of God's activity which would imprison him in a time sequence. Eternity is not simply a very long stretch of time but a totally different quality of existence which we cannot even imagine. I cannot but think that we should have been spared a good deal of theological grief if some of our worthy divines had borne that fact in mind.

But I am sure it does prove this (and here I become biblical as well as philosophical): the only temporal word which really has any relevance in our relationship to God is *now*. If we take advantage of it, the past of which we are only too painfully aware disappears and the future, which has already been realized in Jesus Christ, ceases to be uncertain. Foreknowledge is a poor thing compared with the certainty, "I know even as I am known."

Sincerely,

19

DEAR JAN,

I must confess I was glad to read in your letter that you were willing to lay speculation to one side and raise a question which is somewhat more answerable. You are not the first person to raise it. And I admit it would seem reasonable to suppose that those who believe in election and predestination would forthwith cease all moral endeavor. If God has chosen me and nothing can alter his choice, why should I bother? Isn't that a logical question?

James Anthony Froude, whom I quoted to you earlier, had you in mind apparently when he wrote that letter to Charles Kingsley.

> I object altogether to arguing against doctrine on the ground that such and such things *must* follow. They may with this and that person. The old pagan Irish were afraid of Christianity, because it preached the acceptance of repentance. They said if repentance is accepted men will sin freely and will say, I will repent and all will be well. They were wrong. So will every one be who judges of truth or falsehood by what *must* be the moral results from it.*

I don't want to dwell on Froude's remarks except to say that I think they are a healthy reminder, especially to Americans for whom the pragmatic argument is usually the paramount one, that "Is it true?" is a more important question than "What does it produce?" There have been

* Dunn, *James Anthony Froude*, p. 191.

cases, I am told, of moral lassitude, not to say moral disgrace, resulting from a zealous belief in election. But even if these cases numbered into the thousands, we should still be faced with the question of truth.

But the fact is that they have never numbered into the thousands. The fact is that a belief in predestination has almost never produced the result you suggest. Take a broad survey of Reformation Protestantism and see what you find. In such diverse places as Holland, Switzerland, Huguenot France, Scotland, and New England the Protestants were passionate believers in election. Would you say from what you know of their history that any or all of these groups were marked by moral indifference?

Well, of course not. A group of busier bees it would be hard to imagine. In fact, the irony of it all is that the very group of people who by your logic should be guilty of moral indifference is in point of fact the group of people whom many of our contemporaries accuse of an overly active moral scrupulosity! The moral sensitivities of Scottish Presbyterians or New England Puritans, to go no further, were famous—not to say notorious!

You have not asked the question, but I should like to throw it in here anyway. It is no less amazing, I think, that these same people who could have rested securely in the knowledge of their election became leaders in social responsibility. In England they still speak of the "nonconformist conscience." "The New England conscience" is something of a byword with us. Well, in either case that conscience was the product of this same doctrine. Instead of resting in their own spiritual security and ignoring the social and political evils around them, the elect have always moved mightily to change the surrounding situation.

But I don't really think this is as much of a puzzle as it may seem. The Reformation solved the puzzle long ago. To be sure, it was then posed in a somewhat different form. If good works have nothing to do with salvation, why do them? And the Reformation answer was clear and simple: out of gratitude. I am afraid that much of our modern Protestantism misses this. Though in very different terms from the Middle Ages, we still think in terms of rewards. You would be surprised at the number of intelligent people who think that because they go to church every Sunday, say their prayers, and don't injure their neighbors, they should be immune to gallstones! "I am good because I expect some return from it" is still viable Protestantism, it would seem.

But not Reformation Protestantism! "I am good because I am thankful." When I survey what God has done, is doing, and is yet to do for me in Jesus Christ, how can I ever express my thanks except in the way of obedient service! This was how the elect felt. That was what drove them out into the hard business of moral living and even, I like to think, social reform. Belief in election, to answer your question, so far from cutting the moral nerve, gives it new life by nourishing it with the powerful stream of gratitude.

I should like to let my answer rest there. But I think there is probably something more to be said. I'll take that up in my next letter.

Sincerely,

20

DEAR JAN,

Of course you wondered what that something more could be. Well, did you ever notice the curious way in which the Bible states both sides of the predestination question at once? I think of two illustrations almost immediately. Our Lord once said, "All that the Father gives me will come to me; and him who comes to me I will not cast out." There is the paradox of God's choice and man's response, not in cooperation, but in tension.

Paul put it even more dramatically. "Work out your own salvation with fear and trembling," he wrote to his friends in Philippi, "for God is at work in you, both to will and to work for his good pleasure" (2:12-13). I am not now concerned to try to explain this paradox. In fact, I do not think it can be explained. I call it to your attention simply to underscore the fact that while the Scriptures leave no room for doubt that grace is God's free gift, they also leave no room for doubt that the demand for grateful obedience is laid upon those to whom God has given this gift.

In fact, despite the perseverance of the saints (which was never, I am sure, meant to be interpreted immorally), do we not have to admit that the New Testament is filled with warnings about the possibility of losing our calling and election? To go no further, Israel certainly lost hers! And to what purpose are all the admonitions in Scripture about *enduring to the end* if this is not a real possibility?

Our failures effect no change in God's love and forgiveness. But they can (and alas sometimes do) effect changes in our willingness and ability to receive and accept that love and forgiveness. No man had a more fervent belief in God's election than the apostle Paul. When he wrote to his congregations, he was writing to the elect. He called them such. Yet look at what a large portion of every one of his letters is given over to straight ethical exhortation.

I mention all this because it seems to me to be part of the full answer to your question about the relationship of predestination to morality. I think I should have to say that just as the reprobate will be known only at the end of history, so, in a certain sense, will the elect. To be sure, any man who knows himself to be in a living relationship with Christ can be certain of his election, whatever may be his lapses. But that relationship can be empty pretense so far as his neighbors are concerned.

Gratitude is certainly the great motive for Christian living. But can we rule out entirely this other motive, the desire to make our calling and election sure, the earnest intention to continue to the end? I think not. I have to admit that many times it has been perverted and abused. The line between the motive and that of piling up a good record to win a reward is not always a clear one. But there is such a line of demarcation. If no less a person than Paul could envision the possibility, after preaching to others, of himself being disqualified (I Cor. 9:27), we certainly cannot dismiss "working out our own salvation" as an unworthy motive for ourselves.

But never forget the other half of the paradox. That would be fatal. Even as we work out our own salvation in the day-to-day decisions of existence, it is God who is at work in us. And he works in us, please notice, to do his will. If that were not so, the mess would be worse than it is! History is strewn with the wreckage of the salvations men have tried to work out for themselves—some of them pretty bloody ones too.

I should like to underscore what I said rather parenthetically at the beginning of this letter. None of this means some kind of divine-human cooperation, as though we went as far as we could and then God came along graciously to supply the deficiency. He does everything. But it is exactly the marvel of his omnipotence that he does it, through his Spirit, in terms of our decisions, our actions, our responses. No man can so much as say "Jesus is Lord" without the influence of the Spirit. But still, once it is said, it is the man who says it and not some heavenly ventriloquist!

Perhaps the elect are not aware of this paradox. But certainly any man who has come through some dark valley with his faith unshaken and his trust unbroken has to say, "Surely the Lord was in this place, though I did not know it."

Sincerely,

21

Dear Jan,

It does seem hard to believe that the summer is almost over, doesn't it? It seems harder for me to believe that you can be running out of questions about our problem. Well, cheer up; I am not out of answers! At least, I have several observations left to make. And since none of your comments seems to have elicited them, I shall make them anyway—at least so long as the vacation holds out.

The first is one which I feel I should have made long ago. So let me make it now as startlingly as I can. I sometimes think that one of the chief troubles with every discussion of predestination which I have read is its implicit Unitarianism. Of course, I know that not one of these authors was really Unitarian. But in a strange way all of them seem to ignore the basic truth that God is in three persons; they all write as though election were a decree of an isolated Omnipotence and not the purpose of Father, Son, and Holy Spirit.

If I were to write a systematic theology, I should like to try to rethink the doctrine of predestination from a Trinitarian point of view. At least in these few remaining letters let me indicate some of the points which I think it should include.

I will begin with the fact of which Karl Barth recently has made a great deal: election is *in Christ*. Actually Luther and Calvin, though they looked at it from different standpoints, both said almost the same thing. "Christ is the mirror of election." I think I know what they meant.

So often when we speak about salvation we think of it in rather abstract terms, as the negative of damnation, as that to which, through election, willy-nilly, we are whisked by some divine decree.

But salvation means to be *in Christ*. And to be *in Christ* is God's purpose in election. It is this, as Paul says over and over again, to which he has predestined us. So long as we speak about *election* or *predestination,* we are talking abstractions. The moment we begin to speak about Christ, our abstraction begins to take on specific form. I have the suspicion that much of our problem with predestination arises from the abstraction. The specific takes away many of our problems.

For to be *in Christ* is both present reality and future goal. It is present reality in that even the desperate hand reached out in trust is taken in mercy. The most hopeless specimen of humanity who cries out "Lord, have mercy" is in Christ, is in the company of the elect. There is the present reality.

But that, if I may say it reverently, is not the full dimension of our destiny. "Beholding the glory of the Lord, we are changed into his likeness from one degree of glory to another." There is the future goal. That our stubborn, sinful, proud human nature in all of the contradictions of existence is being transformed into the image and likeness of Christ—nothing less than this is the miracle of the gospel. Though we are the sons of God, it does not yet appear what we shall be except that the final product shall be like him.

It is our election *in Christ,* I think, which helps to explain the mystery we discussed a little while ago, the paradox that election is both an accomplished reality and a continuing process: accomplished reality insofar as God's mercy in Christ has been freely given to us, continuing process insofar as our transformation into the image of

Christ is going on all the days of our life. There is thus a real sense in which we can say, "I have been elected" and "I am being elected."

Once you see this, I think it does a great deal to help the common notion that election is nothing but the carrying out in time of a decision which God made (it is a great temptation to say "millions of years ago" but you know what is wrong with that) in eternity. It is that, of course; and if God had not made that decision, we should have little to talk about. But that decision which God made in eternity may require an entire lifetime for its execution. If I may say it theologically, to be elect in Christ involves not only justification but also sanctification, not only acceptance but also growth and transformation.

There are many other aspects to it, of course. But I think you can see the one which I am trying to stress. To be among the elect is not simply to be God's arbitrary darling. To be among the elect is to be in Christ; and that means we have a final goal, purpose, and destiny which all the years of our lives are not sufficient to fulfill.

Sincerely,

22

DEAR JAN,

Did my last letter really add a dimension to this idea of predestination of which you had never thought? Well, hang on; perhaps in this letter I can succeed in adding another!

For just as we cannot really talk about election unless we add the phrase *in Christ,* so I maintain, we cannot discuss election in Christ unless we add the further phrase *through the Holy Spirit.* In fact, have we not noticed this lack all throughout our correspondence? Time and again we have said that one of the weaknesses in the popular (and orthodox) conception of predestination is the way in which it supposes that God intervenes in our lives by ignoring or even destroying our own powers of mind and heart and spirit.

Now I do not want to overestimate these powers, for they are sinful powers, as much ravaged by our depravity as the rest of us. But they are the theater, so to speak, in which the Spirit of God dwells and works. And unless we include the Spirit working there, influencing us to our acceptance of God's mercy in Christ, God's redemption is likely to remain something outside us. I can easily see how a man might think that since election is in Christ, his duty is to follow the Sermon on the Mount, obey the Golden Rule, or some such thing. In fact, I have a great many parishioners who do think this way, even if election has never crossed their minds.

But the following of an external law, whether reluctant

or enthusiastic, is a far cry from the inner transformation of the personality until it begins to conform to that law. That is why we dare not forget the role of the Spirit in predestination. Between God's demand and our acceptance of that demand, he is in every sense the vital link. The power that reshapes our proud desires and purposes into conformity with God's desires and purposes is the Holy Spirit. Without him the whole story simply makes no sense.

In fact, I think I can go even further. How do we recognize that that abject figure hanging on his cross is God's mercy extended to us in our need? How are we made to see that Christ is the real pattern of our existence? Surely not by any clever divination of our own; certainly not by any prudential human reckoning. It is the Spirit in our hearts who makes us see Christ in the crucified man of Nazareth. It is the Spirit in our hearts who makes us see the real purpose of our lives in that figure of ancient history whom, even in our best moments, we should otherwise put in the same category as Socrates or Buddha. If you doubt me, see what happens to Jesus when the world which does not know the Spirit tries to account for him!

I suppose I should not be surprised at the neglect of the Holy Spirit at this point. It is, after all, only one with the neglect of him at almost every point in contemporary religion. Somehow we have let him become the exclusive property of the various Pentecostal sects, associating him with such outlandish things as speaking with tongues or rolling on the floor. But whatever may be the case elsewhere, in the doctrine of predestination, it is fatal if he be left out of consideration.

That he has been is amply proven by the fact that most of us think of predestination as some massive scheme concocted in eternity to be dropped on us in time. The whole subjective realization of God's design, its internal appropriation, so to speak, depends entirely upon the work of the Spirit. Leave him out and the whole thing seems monstrous or simply makes no sense. But include him in his vital role and then what God has purposed becomes understandable through his ministry to us.

Indeed, it seems to me that what I have been trying to say is nothing but a further extension of something which was very precious to the Reformation—the inner witness of the Holy Spirit. The Reformers all remind us that it is this witness which establishes the authority of the Word in our hearts. Well, is this not something of a parallel case? Just as the Word becomes authoritative for me only when I read it under the guidance of the Spirit and am persuaded of its truth by him, so predestination becomes authoritative for me only in the same way and under the same auspices. It is not my choice but the Holy Spirit's guidance which brings me to accept my election in Christ.

Sincerely,

23

Dear Jan,

Yes, I agree. What I had to say in the last letter ought to be at least a sermon and perhaps even a book. But since I have no time for either right now, you will let me go on to the last thing I have to say. Even though you may think that after all these letters there is nothing left to say about the Father and predestination, let me try to say it anyway.

Can you guess why I have kept this discussion till last? It is because I want to discuss the role not of God, who can easily be a philosophical or theological abstraction (and too often, I fear, is), but because I want to discuss the role of the Father. There is a difference. We could conceivably know God through unaided human reasoning. But we know the Father only through Christ and the Spirit. "No one comes to the Father," said our Lord, "but by me." That is not religious bigotry; it is sober fact.

Once again let me say that the discussion about predestination, as it seems to me, has often got off on a wrong foot because it starts from God—undefined. This flaw is to be found even in some of our classic Christian confessions. But as Christians we can never start any discussion from God undefined. We can start them only from the Father who is the Father not because of any sentimental foolishness about the fatherhood of God and the brotherhood of man, but because he is the Father of Jesus Christ.

That election is the will of the Father, it seems to me,

puts a stop to all suggestions that God's choice is based upon some foreseen goodness in the lives of those whom he chooses. The base is entirely wrong. Because it is the choice of the Father, the only reason behind it is love, not love in the sense of general (and often useless) benevolence but love as displayed by Christ. So long as we interpret predestination in terms of love, as surely *in Christ* we are entitled to do, we are on safe ground.

Now the fact that God is indeed Father is perhaps nowhere better proved than in the idea of predestination. If he were simply, as we so often say, the creator and preserver of the universe, election in Christ conceivably might never have happened. I do not know how, but I am sure that the good order of the universe could somehow have been preserved without all of this unnecessary fussing with man. It is just because God has chosen to deliver man from his mess—a choice of which we should have no awareness apart from Jesus Christ, apart from the Bible—that we can say *Father*. It is election with all that follows from it in the way of mercy, forgiveness, and redemption that reveals the creator and preserver of the universe as indeed "our Father."

But before I leave this whole topic I should like to point out how very important it is to keep the Trinity in the whole picture of predestination. Emphasize the work of the Father (or more accurately God), as has often been done, and predestination becomes a coldly impersonal and arbitrary scheme imposed upon a humanity which has nothing to say about it and nothing to do with it. A predestination which is the work of the creator and preserver is pure executive fiat and nothing more.

If, on the other hand, you play up predestination as the work of Christ (which, without going into detail, is the fashion of some of our modern theologians) you may avoid the fatalism and necessitarianism which goes with the first exaggeration but not without creating some new problems. Not only can such a view of predestination easily lead to universalism, it can just as easily lead to the blurring of all moral distinctions. An easy forgiveness takes away the urgency to work out our own salvation, to make our calling and election sure.

And I can easily see how a predestination which depended entirely on the Holy Spirit (though I must confess I have never met with such a thing) could become a subjective rampage. I suppose the wild excesses of the early Quakers is the nearest thing to it. Whatever I chose to be or to do could be justified on the basis that the Spirit told me so.

Well, I have merely sketched in an outline. But it has been enough, I hope, to persuade you that predestination makes sense only when we remember that God is Father, Son, and Holy Spirit.

Sincerely,

24

DEAR JAN,

Do you realize that in a few days I shall be home again? In fact, the mails being what they are, I may very well be back before this letter. So let me wind up this correspondence by making a suggestion or two and then trying to summarize what we have said. If there are any loose ends, we can discuss them when we see each other very shortly.

The suggestion that I have wanted to make several times in this correspondence but never known quite when to do it is this. Because of a long historical, philosophical, and even religious conditioning, we tend to think of this whole question of election and predestination in very individual terms. What has God decided for me, for my wife, for my children?

At this late date I don't know how we can change that. But as I read the New Testament it comes to me with increasing clarity that Paul never thought in our terms. His ideas of election and predestination were always in terms of a community, Israel or the church. I have not checked every reference but I don't remember one in which he says "God predestined *me*." It is always "God predestined *us*." Nor do I think that is an editorial plural (no, nor a royal one either!). I think he quite sincerely meant the church. I don't think he ever thought about the matter in our individual terms.

I don't exactly know where this takes us. Certainly it is almost impossible at this late date to change our style of thought. But just as certainly it ought to be possible whenever we are reading anything the New Testament has to say on the subject to bear this in mind. What was said with reference to a community, a nation, a people is not in all senses perfectly applicable to an individual. I am sure there are many other implications to this, but there is not the time to go into them now.

I have felt several times during our correspondence that you wanted to get into the larger matter of what might be called "providence." Weren't you on the point of asking several times to what extent God controls and directs the everyday events of our lives? I have avoided that topic because it does not really belong in the one which you originally raised. But I think I could say this much, even though it might begin another series of letters next summer! While I do not believe that we are puppets reading a prepared script (nor do I see anything in the Bible requiring us to believe that), I do believe that God, just because he is our Father, uses every event of our lives to persuade us to his will and purpose. This, I take it, is what Paul meant when he wrote that "all things work together for good to them that love God, to them that are the called according to his purpose." Our tragedy, of course, is that we often let our ambitions blind us so that we cannot see what God is seeking to say and do through these events.

Has the time come to summarize our correspondence? I have no carbon copies of it, but I think I can remember the principal things I have tried to say. "He first loved us." There, in a nutshell, is what the idea of predestination wants to say and wants to protect. It stands like a fortress against any attempt to credit our decisions or our choices. They could so easily become "we first loved him." Or worse still, they could so easily become a lever with which we could try to pry favors from God. Our

73